MONEY MOVES

A GUIDE TO CONQUERING COLLEGE DEBT WITH LITTLE FAMILIAL SUPPORT

AMBER PORTER

AMBER PORTER

ISBN: 1977600123
ISBN-13: 978-1977600127

DEDICATION

For my great aunt Christine who thought of me during my most difficult moments, may she rest in peace.

AMBER PORTER

CONTENTS

ACKNOWLEDGMENTS

Thank you to everyone who contributed to my success by giving me kind words and encouragement. Specifically to Michelle Cave who went above and beyond.

1 THIRD PARTY SCHOLARSHIPS

Congratulations, you are already on the path to making money moves towards your goals! Each chapter of this book has much needed information about how to attack the college process. You may have heard a lot of misinformation about loans and how to pay for college. By utilizing the information contained within these chapters, you will be able to attend and complete coursework at a four-year university debt-free. Each chapter gives straightforward and to-the-point advice on how to navigate the process.

There are myriad hacks, tips, and tricks that you can use to maximize your scholarship potential. Before researching any scholarships, start by writing your personal statement. The key to winning any award or getting scholarship money is a riveting personal statement, which is required in almost every application. You should spend as much time as possible perfecting this statement. This is the single piece of paper that will be the deciding factor between getting the scholarship and receiving a rejection letter. Think critically and deeply about your statement and how you want to depict your life in writing.

The purpose of a personal statement is to tell your story. Your statement needs to describe a pivotal moment in your life. You need to express, in your statement, what it is that drives you to succeed. Your statement should be powerful, concise, and free of errors.

Scholarship committee members are, essentially, trying to bet on who will succeed. There are limited amounts of funds and the committee members are tasked with figuring out who best to receive them. When you are writing your statement you have to think about why someone should fund your education. What about you is so special that someone would want to pay for you to go to college?

The most powerful statements usually come from people who have endured the most struggles. If you have endured a hardship or faced some particular difficulty, you need to write about that experience and describe how it has shaped your life. Some examples include: poverty-related issues, deaths of close family members, losing everything in a fire, being a victim of a crime, traveling to a poverty-stricken area, or doing a mission trip. These are just a few examples of what might make for a powerful statement.

You can write an award winning statement by being descriptive, using colorful language and powerful imagery to depict your story. You need to show your story through your words as opposed to just telling your story. You need to write your statement with such vocabulary, as if to put the reader in your position. Read the following examples and decide which uses colorful language.

Example 1: In the year 2000 my house burned down. It was an awful experience.

Example 2: I walked into my childhood home as tears streamed down my face. The charcoal-like smell overwhelmed my nostrils as I walked through the debris. My childhood, shattered in an instant.

Notice that the second example does not say that the author's house caught fire. However, based on the language, word choices like "charcoal-like smell" and "debris" you can infer that there was a fire. One way to learn to write this way is to imagine the situation as if it were happening at present. Close your eyes and imagine walking through a house where a fire had just been extinguished. What do you smell? What is the ground like as you are walking? What are your thoughts? Is your body reacting- are you crying, shaking? Now try to explain to someone how you feel without actually telling them. If you notice, in example two, the author never says the word "crying." As opposed to example one, example two uses colorful language and depicts the story in a more powerful way.

Once you start to think this way, you will begin to write similarly to example two. If necessary, write your statement normally and then go back and re-construct your sentences with the tips above. You will be surprised by the before and after of your statement.

It may be emotional to write your story. Depending on what you have endured, it can be difficult to provoke old feelings and to bring back old memories. But writing your statement may also give you the ability to get closure.

After you finish writing, spend a lot of time editing your statement for grammar. Your statement should be about two pages in length. Grammatical errors are one of the most common issues with statements. Sentence structure, word choice, and punctuation are common errors also. Ask your high school guidance counselor if they will edit your statement. Also, consider reaching out to your English teacher and ask for any edits. English teachers, oftentimes, have literary backgrounds and can assist you on your descriptive word choice.

Once your statement is edited, it is time to research scholarships. It may be difficult to find out which organizations are offering scholarships to students. The suggestions below are some ideas on where you can find scholarship applications.

Start by getting your high school's scholarship newsletter. These newsletters are extremely valuable because the scholarships listed are usually scholarships that past students have received. You should look carefully at all of the requirements and apply to all of the scholarships for which you are eligible. These newsletters may also reveal high school funded scholarships. The high school that I attended gave two, 250-dollar, scholarships to high school seniors each year.

Some well-established religious institutions offer scholarships to youth. Check with local religious institutions to see if you can apply. Some institutions require that you be a member before receiving a scholarship. Consider joining one of these institutions for scholarship applicability.

Local sororities and fraternities provide scholarships for the communities where they serve. For example, both Alpha Kappa Alpha and Delta Sigma Theta offered significant scholarships in my community. Those organizations pride themselves on service and are willing to give scholarships to those from the community who are in need. Scholarship applicants typically have to go through an interview process wherein they have to recite principles of the organization and show knowledge of famous members of the sorority. It is important that you research and prepare extensively for these interviews.

There are many college specific scholarships as well. I suggest visiting the website for the college that you will be attending. Find the scholarships portion of the website and apply for all of the scholarships available for rising or incoming freshman.

There are several restaurants and department stores that give students scholarships yearly. The founders of Wal-Mart created the Sam Walton Foundation. Each year this foundation gives scholarships to youth who meet certain criteria. Similarly, McDonalds, Burger King, Coca-Cola and BP gas stations give scholarships to high school students. Check the websites of these businesses for more information about their scholarship requirements.

Google will be your greatest ally in finding scholarships. I suggest literally searching "scholarships for high school juniors/seniors" or "most popular scholarships" and applying for all scholarships for which you meet the requirements. Bill and Melinda Gates, for example, have one of the largest scholarship programs. It may be exhausting to constantly search Google, but it is very necessary. You can then make a list of all of the scholarships and apply to them if you are eligible.

When doing so many scholarship applications, be careful not to mix up any deadlines or requirements. I suggest getting a student planner and calendaring the dates for when the scholarships are due. Make sure to mail the applications at least a week in advance of the deadline. Read the eligibility requirements carefully and make sure that you are eligible to apply. Take note about what attachments are needed to submit a completed application. Some scholarship applications require that you attach your transcript or a letter of recommendation.

You may be wondering how you will be able to afford the costs of copying and sending the materials. You may also be wondering how bothersome it might be to get so many letters of recommendation for each scholarship. I have a few suggestions to solve these problems. First, most high schools will mail completed scholarship applications for free. They will -fax them for free most times. You should speak to your high school guidance counselor about this. Most scholarships will also request an official transcript be submitted, which may be costly. You should request one official transcript and make several copies of it. This will solve the problem of paying for multiple transcripts. Again, look closely at the scholarship requirements, if the scholarship requires that the transcript be sealed than obviously do not send them one of your copies. If all the scholarship application requires is a transcript, and does not give any additional requirements or notes about the transcript, you should be safe sending the copy.

Letters of recommendation may be hard to gather. You should find three teachers, faculty members, or coaches that view you in a positive light. You should ask if they can write you a general recommendation letter for scholarships. If they agree, have them address it "to whom it may concern." Ask them if they will give you their permission to copy the letter and send it to any scholarships for which you are eligible. If they agree, make several copies of their letters and add them to all of your applications that require a letter of recommendation. By streamlining the process, already having your personal statement done, letters of recommendation copied, and copies of transcripts, you will be able to apply for more scholarships in a shorter amount of time.

To further streamline the process, make a folder and put copies of your personal statement, letters of recommendation, and transcript in it. You should have this folder ready to use at all times. That way, when you are ready to apply for scholarships you are just stuffing envelopes.

Ask your school's guidance office if they will allow you to make copies of these items free of charge. If you explain you need the copies for scholarship applications, the school should allow you to make limited copies. Moreover, I suggest doing your applications in the school's guidance office. The staff there may be able to assist you if you get stuck doing an application.

You should spend as much of your free time as possible doing scholarship applications. You should spend all of your free periods at the library or guidance office. If you use the above tips, it should not take you a long time to do the applications. I suggest that you apply to at least one hundred scholarships. This will maximize your chances of receiving scholarship funds.

Many people have made comments to me about how my race likely played a big part in my ability to receive scholarships. This is one of the biggest misconceptions. Typically when you receive a scholarship you are invited to a scholarship dinner. You are able to meet all of the people who also received the same scholarship. I went to all of my scholarship dinners and met my fellow scholarship recipients. More than seventy percent of the scholarships that I received had recipients that were white males. It is a completely false assumption that only minorities are able to receive scholarships in the United States.

I had a conversation with one of my white female friends in college about a similar issue. She was considering applying for a diversity scholarship at our college. She was concerned that she would not get the scholarship because she wasn't a minority. I encouraged her to apply since the scholarship was for students who facilitated diversity in higher education. I told her that I believed that she met the requirements of the scholarship. My friend had made great efforts to encourage diversity and frequently attended cultural group meetings and events. She did apply for that scholarship, and that year she was awarded a 5,000-dollar diversity scholarship.

Applying for scholarships is exhausting. However, using

14

the methods outlined above will almost guarantee that you get a scholarship, assuming you have a great personal statement and follow the suggestions above as closely as possible. You will not get the scholarships that you don't apply for. I repeat, you will not get a scholarship that you did not apply for. People often complain about how they didn't receive any scholarships, and those people are usually people that did not apply for any scholarships. For some reason, people expect to get scholarships handed to them. Everyone is mediocre unless proven otherwise. If you want your education paid for, you have to work extremely hard to prove yourself worthy. You have to show the scholarship committee members that you are extraordinary. You have to show the committee that you will succeed. This process requires an abundance of time, energy, and effort. If you are willing to put in the work, you will see a reward. If you are not willing to put an adequate amount of time into this process, do not complain later about not receiving funding.

2 NEGOTIATION STRATEGIES

Colleges are very competitive and you can use that to your advantage. When applying for college, do not just apply to one or two schools. I suggest applying to ten or more schools. You should apply to reach, match and safety schools. Make sure to apply to enough safety schools to maximize your scholarship/financial aid potential.

Don't worry about the fees associated with applying to numerous colleges. If you do not have the money, most colleges will give you a fee waiver. You can call the college or visit their website to see if you meet the requirements for the application fee waiver. Even if you do not meet the requirements you can still call the college and ask if they will make an exception. If this does not work, I would still suggest applying to colleges in mass. This is an investment in your future that will eventually save you money.

After you are accepted to a college, you will receive a financial aid package or award letter. On the award letter it will tell you all of the funding you are able to receive, this will probably include merit scholarships, need-based scholarships and any other government assistance grants and loans (assuming you completed the FAFSA application in the United States). Start by adding up all of the scholarship/grant money, and do not include the loans. Use that award amount to negotiate with the other schools where you were accepted. You will then need to call the admissions office at the schools that offered you lower scholarship awards and ask them to match your award from the school with the highest award.

For example, if you applied to Harvard University and they offered you a 5,000-dollar merit scholarship and a 10,000-dollar need-based scholarship, your total award amount would be 15,000-dollars at Harvard. Let's say you also applied to Northwestern University and they offered you a 20,000-dollar merit scholarship and 5,000-dollar need-based scholarship, your total award amount would be 25,000-dollars at Northwestern. Assuming these are the only schools where you gained admission, you would then call the admissions department at Harvard and ask that they match your 25,000-dollar award package from Northwestern.

17

This may sound crazy, but most schools are so competitive that they will either match your award or raise the scholarship amount that they awarded to you previously. Admissions departments, oftentimes, have large latitude in what they can offer students. There are often additional funds available for the year that goes unused.

It is important to call the schools and be prepared to negotiate. Confidence is key during negotiations. Explain to the school that you are very interested in their program and give reasons why you would prefer to go to that school over your other choices. Explain that, financially, the school with the higher scholarship is alluring since the costs of college are rising yearly, but that you don't want your inability to afford their great school to hinder your ability to attend. Be careful not to mention any third party scholarships that you may receive. Talk to the admissions office as if the only funding you will receive is from their institution.

Be prepared to talk about yourself and how you would be a key asset to the institution. Obviously, do not overdo it and appear to be conceited, but at the same time do not be humble. Many students make the mistake of thinking that their personal statement or grades will speak for them. This is a misconception. You are a high school student and have not made a name for yourself yet. You need to advocate for yourself.

If you are not accustomed to advocating for yourself, think of three great strengths that you possess and argue that those skills will be a value to the learning institution. Think carefully about your strengths and how those might relate to the mission statement of the college.

If you do not feel like you have any strengths, be creative. Did you work a part-time job during high school? Working may show your ability to multi-task. Many college students struggle with juggling their classwork and new life responsibilities without parents. This can cause many students' grades to drop. If you have worked a part-time job during high school, it may show that the college transition will be easier for you, and that you will be able to maintain good grades. Additionally, any leadership or extracurricular activities that you have participated in while in high school may be beneficial. Did you serve on a church youth group board or participate in a private volleyball team? These are examples of things to mention while negotiating with college admissions.

Do not be afraid to negotiate. The college will not revoke your offer or scholarship if you call and politely ask for them to consider giving you more funding. Unless you are being a complete jerk to the admissions department, the worse thing that they can do is deny your request. Do not be afraid to assert yourself and go after what you want in life.

3 TUITION & FEES

In order to truly conquer college debt, a critical review of your college's tuition and fees is necessary. Let's start with tuition. When you receive your financial aid package in the mail, it should give you not only a list of awards (scholarships, loans, grants), but also a list of the costs of attendance. Don't forget that tuition increases yearly. Thus, your 5,000-dollar scholarship may not be of the same value when tuition increases an additional 2,000-dollars your second year. One suggestion is to ask your college if they will lock in your tuition. That means that your tuition will remain the same for all four years of your attendance. This will prevent you from being blindsided when tuition increases your second year. Some colleges will do this automatically and others will not. This is definitely something to consider when speaking with college admissions departments.

Fees are very tricky and you can save thousands of dollars by carefully reviewing which fees are mandatory and which are optional. Firstly, consider skipping the meal plan. Most colleges will add a significant fee for a semester-long meal plan, usually 1,500-2,500 dollars per semester. Depending on what sort of housing you receive, the meal plan is optional. For example, if you are living in an off-campus apartment you may not need a meal plan. It may be daunting learning how to cook, if you don't already know how, but plenty of college students live off of ramen and frozen pizza and you can too. Imagine you spend 200-dollars per month on groceries. There are five months in a semester. Thus, at 200-dollars per month, you would spend 1,000-dollars per semester on groceries. This is cheaper than getting the meal plan.

Additionally, most states in the U.S have supplemental nutrition assistance programs. These programs require that you work at least twenty hours per week and that you, individually, live below the poverty line to qualify (this may vary state to state). The program gives you a set amount of money to spend per month on food items in grocery or department stores. The government funding is loaded onto a card and you can use that card at your leisure throughout the month. Utilizing this program can save you 3,000-5,000-

dollars per year.

Also optional is the health insurance fee. First and foremost, I am NOT suggesting that anyone go without health care. However, health insurance laws in the United States allow for a youth to stay on their parent's health insurance until twenty-six-years-old. The college that you will attend will automatically give you an insurance plan with your tuition and add the fee to your bill. Usually you can opt out of this plan and fee if you show proof that you already have health insurance through your parents or otherwise.

There may be other optional fees included in your bill. The best way to combat unnecessary fees is to have a meeting with a financial services member and ask about opting out of optional fees.

4 WORK SMART

Conquer debt by not taking out any cost of living loans. The cost of living loans that students take out during college are a large percentage of their student debt. Instead of relying on a financial aid refund check, work a part-time job. The best job to get while in college is a job at the library or a front desk job at one of the offices or the dorms. Those jobs allow students to multi-task to a large degree. Student workers are typically allowed to work on their homework and other assignments during work hours. Working at the library is perfect for this because it is so quiet. There are probably only a few times during a shift at the library that a student worker is interrupted. Most student workers at the school library are only there in case someone has a question about how to find a certain book. This means that you will have the majority of the shift to get your homework and projects done.

Likewise, a dorm front desk or an office front desk job is also helpful. Front desk staff are responsible for answering phones and giving directions to people who come in and ask. This again provides the student with a lot of the time to get their homework done.

Be careful, because there are some on-campus jobs that do not allow for as much free time. Some jobs at the library require students to stock or unload items on shelves. Do not apply for these positions. Do not do a job where you have to work more than fifty percent of the time that you are there. There are plenty of jobs that you can do that will allow you to do the minimum amount of work and still have time to get your assignments done.

Consider being a resident assistant/advisor (RA). Generally, you can apply to be a RA after your first year of college. These positions are extremely valuable because you receive free housing and, depending on the college, a free meal plan or a stipend. Resident Assistants are responsible for being in the dorm and mediating roommate disputes. Again, this is another position where you can do your school work whilst being on duty as an RA. For example, if it is your turn to be on duty, meaning you have to stay in the dorm for the night and patrol the halls a few times, you can easily do your homework. Some dorms have study halls, or you can study in your dorm room. You will need to take breaks at some points anyway, and you can take those breaks by patrolling the halls.

Most colleges allow resident assistants to also work a part-time, on-campus job. This will maximize the amount of money you can receive and the amount of time that you will have to study.

The jobs described above are very coveted, and therefore may be hard to obtain. Worst-case scenario, you work a job in retail. This is recommended only as a last resort. These jobs are particularly risky because your employer will not care about your class schedule. You will have to give your employer your schedule and probably constantly remind them that you have class. School is your first priority; otherwise this is all pointless. If you absolutely cannot get an on-campus job then you should work a retail job. I would suggest finding a retail job that will, at least, have some sort of added bonus or benefit. For example, my freshman year of college I worked at a Starbucks in a hotel. The hotel provided their workers with free meals in the break room. You could get sandwiches, beverages, hamburgers and whatever the special was for that day. This was helpful since I did not have a meal plan at the time and I could go there for meals. Some other retail stores, most mobile phone companies, will offer tuition assistance. The aforementioned benefits are what to look for when searching for a retail job.

It is important that you strictly manage the money you receive from your job. Half of the money you earn should go immediately into your savings account. You should live off of the other half. A savings account is necessary because you don't know when you may have an extra expense. In order to avoid debt, you have to be risk-averse. If something happens, like a medical bill or some other cost, you should be able to pay that from your savings account to avoid having to take out a loan.

One other consideration is sleep. You should become accustomed to having six hours of sleep during the school week and eight hours of sleep on the weekends. There are twenty-four hours in a day. If you get only six hours of sleep during the week that will leave you with eighteen hours remaining in the day. Imagine you worked eight hours per day, that would still leave you with ten hours to do your homework, eat, and enjoy your time in college. It is very possible to manage working, coursework, and having fun in college.

5 BOOKS

Conquer debt by minimizing how much you pay for books. Textbooks are hundreds of dollars each semester, and a large cost when calculated in the aggregate. Do not pay for a book if there is no need. During my freshman year of college, I had three roommates and all of us were enrolled in English Composition 101. All of the English Comp classes had the same book. In fact, almost our entire dorm floor was in English Comp 101. Since everyone else bought the book, I didn't see a need for me to buy it also. I switched off borrowing the book from different people on my floor. I was careful not to ask the same person for the book twice so it wouldn't be annoying. It is common for freshman students to be enrolled in similar courses. Consider asking someone from your dorm if they would be interested in sharing a book and splitting the cost.

Moreover, college bookstores usually need help during busy season at the beginning of each semester. Sometimes they will hire students temporarily so they have more staff during this period. Bookstores usually give employee discounts on books and other materials. This is a good way to save money on the books that you do have to buy.

Amazon is also an amazing source when looking to buy books. Amazon offers both new and used books at very low prices. Used books can be great because the prior student that possessed the book may have put helpful notes in the margins. Both new and some used books are eligible for Amazon Prime which means free two day shipping. Amazon also gives students a discounted price for its prime membership.

You can also try to find classes that don't require any books. For one of my electives in college, I took a tai chi course that did not have a required textbook. Colleges usually publish the syllabus from previous semesters. The syllabus will tell you all the information you need to know about the class, including what assignments you will have and the required textbooks.

For classes that do have textbooks, I would suggest asking the professor of the class if you can get away with using an older edition of the textbook. Amazon and other

bookstores will have older editions of required textbooks
severely discounted. Sometimes older editions are very
similar to the newest version.

The library is also a great resource for books. Most
libraries actually have a copy of the latest required textbooks
for rent. These are rented fairly quickly so you should rent
the book as soon as you know that you will be taking the
class. You should be able to use your school ID to rent
books from the library and you can usually rent them for the
entire semester. Likewise, public libraries often have the
same books.

If you do have to buy a book, you should try to sell
it back at the end of the semester. As soon as the class is
over, try to either sell the book back on Amazon or to your
school's bookstore. If you are able to sell your book back
you can then use that money to purchase your new books for
the next semester.

6 THE THREE-YEAR PLAN

You can cut your college costs immensely by implementing, what I call, the three-year plan. Finishing your bachelor's degree in three years will cut an entire year of costs from your bill. Additionally, it allows you to get to the workplace faster to start making money- or to graduate school. Completing the three-year plan is not easy, but it is definitely possible.

If you want to do this, you have to be extremely strategic about how you plan out your course load. In order for this to work, you have to say goodbye to summer. During the summer, apply for admissions at a community college near your home. You should take between six and nine credits every summer. After you take these courses, you can apply for a reverse transfer. That means that you can transfer the community college credits to your bachelor's degree university. You should speak with both your admissions counselor at your bachelor's degree university and the community college's admissions department to ensure that the credits will transfer prior to applying.

Again, be strategic about which classes you are taking. Try to take generic classes that fulfill your general education requirements at the community college. Classes like Intro to Psychology, English 101 and 102, Speech, and Humanities are all fairly easy courses at community colleges. Taking these classes at a community college is much cheaper than taking them at your bachelor's degree university. Community college classes are about one hundred dollars per credit hour, while bachelor's degree universities usually charge 1,000+ dollars per credit hour. Thus, 1,000-dollars can buy you approximately nine credit hours at a community college and approximately one credit hour at a bachelor's degree university. Additionally, most community colleges have programs where you receive free or discounted tuition if you have a certain high school GPA.

Students need about 120 credit hours to get a bachelor's degree. Typically, colleges recommend students take thirty credits per year or fifteen credits per semester to stay on track to graduate in four years. Imagine you wanted to complete the three-year plan. If you took nine credit hours or three classes the summer between high school and college, another nine credit hours the summer between your first and second year of college, and then another nine credits between your second and third year of college; you would have an additional twenty-seven credit hours. Assuming you could pick up three additional credits during any semester of college, you would then be set to graduate at the end of your third year.

I realize that some students may not want to start college immediately upon graduating high school. That is understandable. Even assuming you only took summer classes for two summers, you would still have an additional twelve to eighteen credit hours, which would knock off an entire semester of tuition, fees, and housing from your bill.

Besides taking summer classes, there are other ways to get extra credits and do the three year plan. Another way to do the three-year plan is to take more credits during the semester. Each college has a maximum credit limit allowable per semester. College guidance counselors will try to convince you to take twelve or fifteen credits per semester. What they don't tell you is that you are actually paying for the maximum credit limit. At Boston University, for example, each student has a maximum credit limit of eighteen credits. That means that the tuition that Boston University students pay for twelve credit hours is the same tuition they pay for eighteen credit hours. You have to remember that colleges are businesses. They want to make money and they will, oftentimes, use scare tactics to get you to take fewer credits per semester. They will tell you that fifteen credits is too many for a freshman to handle and that you should consider taking only twelve. That way, you risk being there for five years and they can charge you for another year's worth of tuition and fees. The first semester of freshman year can be difficult. I suggest taking fifteen credits for the first semester and taking the maximum allowable credit hours for each subsequent semesters.

Another way to get some extra credits during the semester is to request a course overload. This request, if granted, will allow you to take additional credits during the semester for a small fee. Some colleges will even waive the fee if you have a good enough reason for the overload. You have to learn to think about this from a financial perspective, taking more credits during the semester is cheaper than paying for a fourth year of college.

You may be wondering how it is possible to take eighteen or more credits per semester. You have to be creative when choosing how to schedule your classes. First, consider taking January term classes. During winter break, most colleges will offer classes. Some of these classes are intensive courses where you go to class every day for a certain amount of hours for two or more weeks. These classes are usually three credits, and are over before the semester starts. Imagine if you took a three-credit class during the January term and then eighteen credits during the regular semester, that would be a total of twenty-one credits for the semester. This is where a course overload form would be useful.

If you are overloading on courses, do not take all of your more difficult classes at once. You should have at least two to three blow off classes each semester. You can find out which classes are blow offs by talking to other students at your college or in your program. You can also check online at ratemyprofessor.com or other blogs about professors. Taking some blow off classes will allow you to focus your time on the more difficult classes. Also, the blow off classes usually require little or no homework, which will allow you more time to work on other things.

Short session classes are also good for getting extra credits during the semester. Short session classes are usually one or two credits but they only last for a portion of the semester. These are great because the class will be complete before finals, again allowing you more time to concentrate on your more difficult classes.

Pay close attention to which classes require a final paper and which require a final exam. Sometimes paper classes can be easier because you know your paper topic/assignment months before the end of the semester. If you complete your paper in advance you will have more time to study for your classes that have final exams.

To conclude, do not finish college in four years, do it in three. You should take at least two summers of classes and then overload during the semester. If you utilize the points made above, you will have 120 credits in no time!

7 USE YOUR HIGH SCHOOL YEARS WISELY

Your high school years are critical to conquering college debt. First of all, your grades and standardized test scores will get you automatic scholarships to college upon application. Colleges give merit scholarships to students who are above certain grade point averages or who have certain standardized test scores. It is imperative that you take high school seriously and get the best grades possible. As far as standardized test scores are concerned, consider hiring a tutor. This may cost a lot of money depending on your location and, therefore, may not be feasible for some students. If you can afford to hire a tutor, or you can somehow gain the assistance of a tutor through special programs in your area, I would highly recommend it. Tutors assist students in raising their standardized test scores, which usually equals more scholarship money from colleges.

Second, high schools give students opportunities to get college credits while in high school. High school students in the United States and Canada can take advanced placement courses, high school classes with college-level curricula. After the class is complete, there is a test given to students. Students with high enough scores on the exam will receive college credit. This will assist you in saving money and utilizing the three-year plan outlined in the previous chapter.

Moreover, other high school classes may offer college credit. Some high schools offer classes that are a joint venture of both the high school and the local community college. These courses typically offer dual, both high school and college, credits. Speak to your high school guidance counselor to find out what classes offer dual credit. If possible, try to take as many college credit classes as possible during high school.

Getting a part-time job in high school is another way to conquer college debt. If possible, try to save one hundred percent of your earnings - this will be extremely helpful in college. With two years of savings, you will be able to pay for any small fees that arise in college, and it will allow for you to have an emergency fund. This savings fund could also pay for any community college classes that you may want to take over the summer after high school or during college. Savings are imperative to conquering debt.

Consider having a college going away party to conquer debt. Some students have going away parties after their high school graduation. This is the time to request all the materials that you may need for college from your friends and family. Unfortunately, most family members will forget about you once you move away for college. They may not realize that you still need school supplies, toiletries, and groceries on a monthly basis. You can solve this problem by creating a registry at stores like Wal-Mart, Target or Costco, and asking your family members to buy you specific items from your list. Consider requesting enough quantities of the items to last you all four (or three) years of college. Ask for things like notebooks, flash cards, paper clips, Xerox paper, flash drives, bedding, body wash, toothpaste and other toiletries. If you know anyone who does extreme couponing, it may be a good idea to contact him or her to do your shopping should you receive monetary gifts. You should also find out which stores are closest to your university. You can then ask your family members for gift cards to those specific stores. Those gift cards can then be used for groceries or other items throughout the semester.

Before going to college, figure out how you will pay your bills. If possible, try to go to college with no bills. Depending on what school you choose, you may not need a car. Most colleges have buses or other forms of transportation to get around campus and to local stores. This will allow you to be free from car payments and car maintenance bills. Consider asking a family member to pay for your cell phone bill throughout college. Most people have family plans and can add you to their plan for a low fee.

High School is a great time to get everything in order. Being prepared is essential to being debt-free.

8 LOANS

Loans are not inherently bad. Student loans are actually considered "good debt" to most financial analysts. The strategies outlined in chapters one through seven are solid strategies to avoid college debt. If you do have to incur some debt, I would suggest keeping that debt to 5,000-dollars or under.

If you qualify for federal student loans (United States), you will not have to pay interest on those loans while you are in school. I would suggest making payments to the loans while you are still enrolled in school. At one point in college, I had to take out a 2,500-dollar loan. I worked multiple jobs at the time. I was able to allocate all of my money from one of the jobs directly to that loan. By the time I graduated college, the loan was completely paid off. Even if you are not able to pay off the loan completely at graduation, paying some money down will decrease the amount of interest you will pay over the lifetime of the loan.

Another option to consider is student loan repayment plans. Depending on what field you will be entering after graduation, it is possible that your industry will be able to pay down some or all of your student loans. For example, some teachers may receive student loan repayment by working in schools that serve low-income families in the United States. Similar programs exist for people in the medical industry. If you do have student loans, it may be good to research these programs before choosing which job you should take.

9 COLLEGE SUPPORT GROUPS

College can be stressful. I cannot guarantee that juggling your college coursework and being debt-free will be easy. Luckily, there are groups that you can join in college that may help you. If you feel stressed or alone consider joining an extracurricular activity. Being a member of a social group can alleviate overwhelming feelings.

There are support groups for first-generation college students. If you are a first-generation college student you may want to talk to other students who are, or have been, in your position. These groups can offer mentoring and funding if you have an emergency or some unmet financial need relating to your tuition and fees.

Religious groups can be helpful in college if you are

affiliated with a religion. These groups offer spiritual support and guidance to students in college. Communicating with like-minded students can help relieve the stresses of life.

Cultural groups are also very popular in college settings. If you are an international student, or have a specific cultural background there are groups that exist to help you feel comfortable. These groups often get together socially to share meals or professionally to help with networking skills.

There will also be groups to join that are specific to your program of study. These groups will often bridge the gap between professors or industry professionals and students. These are helpful groups to join for networking purposes. Also, you can get career advice or internships through these types of groups.

To conclude, do not alienate yourself in college. It is a great benefit to make friends and be social. Extracurricular activities can offer an outlet to students who may need help relieving stress or coping with the day-to-day hardships of college. It is of utmost importance to stay committed to your health and mental wellness. If you don't, you risk experiencing burn out.

10 CONCLUSION

Some of the suggestions in this book seem pretty crazy, but these are all things that I have either actually done, or should have done. I was able to graduate college in three years with no debt and 500-dollars in savings. Additionally, I graduated with honors and finished with a 3.7 GPA. I get many comments on Facebook or other social media outlets from people congratulating my parents for sacrificing their money and their lives so that I could attend college. Many people assume that my parents just wrote checks for my education. That is false. Unfortunately, my parents were not able to help me financially during college. My mother was able to pay my cell phone bill during college, and my parents gave me about one hundred dollars total every year.

It was not easy doing college alone and there were many
dark moments throughout the process, but there was never a
time that I thought I wouldn't succeed. I went through
college as if my life depended on graduating. I wanted to
succeed more than I wanted to breathe. So my question to
you is, how bad do you want it?

I remember sitting in my guidance counselor's office in
high school and applying for scholarships. I would go every
day to that office as soon as it opened in the morning and get
new scholarship applications. I would fill them out there so
that I had people to assist me if I had questions. Growing up,
I didn't know many people who had gone to college, so the
high school guidance counselor employees were the only
people that could help me. One of the many days I was
there, my guidance counselor told me that I should consider
going to a community college for a few years before thinking
of applying to a four-year university. She indicated that if I
couldn't afford college that I shouldn't start by attempting to
get a four-year degree. Her thinking was that I would just
incur debt and make my financial situation worse. I didn't
think much of it at the time. I told her that I wanted to go to
a four-year university and move out of the area and I would
make it happen. At that time, I was taking all honors classes
and was so advanced that I was set to graduate high school a
full year early, yet she told me I should just consider going to

community college. There is absolutely nothing wrong with attending a community college. However, I was an honors student and had the opportunity and desire to attend a four-year university, so why should I have sold myself short?

Looking back, her comment was totally inappropriate. There was absolutely a way for me to go to a four-year university regardless of my financial situation. Instead of giving me more guidance or solutions, she told me not to try. Many do not realize how their words or actions could destroy youth. Youth are far more capable than most people realize. The endurance of young people usually exceeds that of middle aged adults. The ideas I have communicated in this book are very possible for you to achieve.

For some, many things in this book are over the top or unnecessary. Some people would rather have student loan debt than go to these great lengths. Given the student loan debt crisis, I do not agree. Getting a bachelor's degree is a huge investment in your future. Graduating without debt is a major benefit. I truly stand by all of the ideas in this book, the vast majority of which I have done myself.

Lastly, many people call and ask me for advice on financial aid and choosing the right college. I am now doing individualized college counseling for a small fee. Please visit my website for more information.

For more information about how to be debt-free at graduation, visit my website amberporter.weebly.com.

ABOUT THE AUTHOR

Amber Porter is an American lawyer who received her Juris Doctor from the University of Illinois College of Law and her Bachelor of Arts degree from Columbia College Chicago. During both college and law school, Amber received numerous awards for her leadership, service, and commitment to diversity. Amber was able to graduate college, debt-free, in only three short years.

Amber has been practicing law for over three years and spends much of her free time teaching paralegal students legal research and writing at a local community college.

Made in the USA
Lexington, KY
07 October 2017